GEORGE MONOUX'S SCHOOL

Walthamstow
1527-1977

by

C. C. Pond, M.A.(

Vestry House Museum, Vestry Road, London E17 9NH
Monograph (New Series) No. 20
1977
ISBN 085480 035 2

Christopher Pond is an Old Monovian of 1961-68, having been Captain of the School in 1968.

CONTENTS

The illustrations are between pages 22 and 23.

CHAPTER I

GEORGE MONOUX AND THE FOUNDATION OF THE SCHOOL

George Monoux (the Sir was a contemporary courtesy title) was born about 1465, probably the son of Richard Monoux, salter and merchant of London. But it was in Bristol that he first came to note—in 1490 as Bailiff, and in 1501 as Mayor. It is not particularly strange to find Monoux migrating and re-migrating between London and Bristol. He was probably following trade contacts or relations. In 1503, he had returned to London, and was living in Crooked Lane, off Cannon Street. In 1506, he was a Warden of the Drapers' Company, Master in 1506, 1516, 1520, 1526, 1532, and 1539. He was Sheriff of London in 1509, Mayor in 1514 and 1523, and was also elected to Parliament as a Burgess for the City in 1523. There is no doubt that he was exceedingly rich, for he owned land in at least ten counties, besides London.

Part of his landholdings were in Walthamstow and Chingford, and it seems that he made Moones in Billet Road (opposite what is now the McEntee Senior High School) his country residence. One imagines that as he became older, he spent more and more time in Walthamstow, and became less concerned with life in London. Hence his public benefactions were quite naturally applied to Walthamstow. A short list will suffice here. First, he made a causeway and bridge over the Lea Marshes to ease the journey to London. He gave the Parish a Feast Room for the proper celebration of weddings, holy days, and the like, and he paid for the reconstruction of the north aisle of the Parish Church of St. Mary, and of a chantry chapel, gave a folio Bible to the Church, and reconstructed the tower. The endowment of the school and almshouses, for which he is today chiefly remembered, was but one of his public works.

If we put the foundation into historical perspective, it will be seen that the good works of Monoux were but half the story. The almspriest-schoolmaster, in particular, had as his primary duty the singing of prayers in church for Monoux's soul. Such observations were considered of great importance by men of wealth, who regarded them as a means of ensuring their quick passage through Purgatory, and the benefit conferred upon the people by their gifts were, perhaps, subsidiary to this object. Thus it was that on 16th June 1527, Monoux bought from Christchurch Priory, London, the land on which he was to build his almshouses and school. In the conveyance, it is explicitly stated that the purpose of the purchase was the erection of almshouses "and the edification and building for a scole master and a ffree scole as . . . George Monoux, God being his guide, shall devise . . ." Monoux later set out exact details of the accommodation. The schoolmaster's apartments were to measure seventeen feet by fifteen on each of two floors. Similarly, he made rules for the conduct of the master. He was to be of quiet and honest disposition and demeanour, to pray daily for the founder's soul and those of his wives, and, without taking more than his allotted stipend of ten marks (£6 13s. 4d.), was to teach Walthamstow children, but not more than twenty or thirty unless he so wished.

What Monoux did not do was to lay down anything relating to the course of instruction, and this was a cause of great dissent in the ensuing centuries. It is also to be noted that the founder did not specify that the school be a grammar school, that is, a classical school; nor did he, for that matter, exclude classical instruction. But it is doubtful whether he could really have intended it for a wholly classical school; for he could hardly have conceived that 20 or 30 Walthamstow children in a community of about 450 would have needed, or desired, an entirely classical instruction.

For the endowment of the school, Monoux left to trustees on his death (which occurred on 9th February 1544) property off Fenchurch Street in the City, which was let at rents of about £50 p.a. All the school received from that was the master's ten marks, and two marks (26s. 8d.) for the clerk of the Parish, should he assist the master. He appointed several friends and kinsfolk as his trustees. This, again, was rather open to dispute, and the trustees, over the years, obviously took little heed of the needs of the foundation. This is hardly surprising, for their duty had been thrust upon them by accident, and, in all probability, they had no connection with the parish. As the years went by, they had less and less connection with the founder or with his purposes.

CHAPTER II

'DISTANT AND DISHONEST TRUSTEES': 1600-1781

The first account we have of the school functioning is that of 1548, when chantries—that is, arrangements by persons for priests to pray for them after their deaths—were abolished by Henry VIII. In the course of this, the Essex chantries, including the Monoux school-almshouse-chantry charity were recorded. Like virtually every other place in Essex that was visited, Walthamstow is described as a "grate town". The number of its communicants was stated to be about 360, indicating a total population of 450-550. John Hogeson, a man in holy orders, 40 years old, "of goode usage ande conversacion, litterate and teachithe a scole . . ." was Master.

Details of the school's existence in the early seventeenth century are few. The best exposition we have is an Inquisition taken before a jury at Stratford in August 1635. After reciting the Monoux Will, the jurors establish something of the situation in the previous century. It appears that the trustees—the Alfords, who "do pretend to be patrons, and having the placing and displacing of the Schoolmaster", had been negligent in the payment of the master's stipend, and had taken, or encouraged the taking, of fees for the mastership to pass from person to person. They had also, on at least one occasion, appointed a master who was incapable of teaching Latin.

That this should have been raised at all by the jurors indicates strongly that despite the lack of guidance from the founder, the school did in the seventeenth century normally teach Latin. The later Commission which required the master to be able to teach the classics was not, therefore, doing any more than reinforcing the status quo. Indeed, an early seventeenth century master, Leonard Taylor, was evidently an elderly doctor of divinity from Oxford of some repute; and the position obviously commanded some prestige when a master paid his predecessor £20 for the succession to the mastership. Most of these masters, we may presume, would have taken private pupils—probably not many—to supplement their income. This was not forbidden by the statutes, and was a common practice.

The trustees had also, according to the 1635 jury, not maintained the buildings . . . "the said schoolhouse, almshouse and chapel [i.e. the Monoux chapel in St. Mary's Church] now are, and for the space of these twenty years last past, have been much ruined, and in great decay for want of necessary repairs".

Unfortunately, we have little idea of whether the 1635 inquisition helped rectify the trustees' mismanagement. It is probable that it did not, for in March 1659, another inquisition was held, this time at

Leytonstone, and the familiar grumbles were recited about delays in repairing the building, failures to pay stipends promptly, and depriving the almspeople of their rights. It was in this case that the judgement of the Commissioners laid down that when the mastership fell vacant, the trustees should "for ever hereafter . . . putt and place in the said schole one able scholar, that shal be a graduate, and hath taken the degree of Batchelour of Art in one of the Universities of Oxford or Cambridge, and shal be able to teach the Greeke and Latine tongues". His stipend was increased to £20 per annum, and that of the Parish Clerk to £3 6s. 8d.

The Commission of 1659 was important because it suggested that the school was to be regarded as a Grammar School, rather than as a free school of low status; which interpretation was perfectly acceptable under Monoux's ordinances. The Essex Victoria County History suggests that the Commission was not obeyed, but from those names of masters appointed in the ensuing years which have survived, it does seem that graduates were insisted upon, though from Trinity, Dublin, as well as Oxford and Cambridge. Numbers in the school were doubtless very low, and almost certainly the private pupil from outside would have figured in the scene.

Henry Maynard is one of the school's benefactors whose name is all but forgotten in its annals. He augmented the charity, however, by about 50% of its original value, and gave outright the sum of £50 for repairs. This may not seem much, yet at the time cottages were being built in Walthamstow for £16 each. Maynard died in 1686, but there was trouble in obtaining the legacy from his executors. This led to yet another Commission, held at the Green Man, Leytonstone, on 8th June 1699. At that time, only £37 10s. 0d. had been paid out of the £50 (and that not until 1698), and none of the rest. This time the executors were ordered to pay, with costs.

It was probably with the Maynard £50, and, no doubt, some money from the Parish, that the building was reconstructed. The Royal Commission on Historical Monuments estimated that this took place about 1700, and at this time the extension of the lower storey on the west wing was removed. The next major alterations did not take place until 1815.

Maynard's will provided also that his executors and their heirs be empowered to nominate eight children to the school at any one time, and this was carried out regularly over the ensuing 120 years.

CHAPTER III

CONTROL BY THE PARISH : 1782-1819

In the seventeenth century, as we have seen, the charity was often openly denied its legitimate funds, and, for this reason, records relating to it have survived. In the eighteenth century, we have no such records, which may indicate that the situation improved somewhat. But we cannot say so for certain. There are no records at all of the school between the 1699 inquisition and 1781, from which fact the most probable deduction is that the school maintained a quiet and unspectacular existence.

On 1st July 1781, the Vestry appointed a committee to negotiate with the Monoux trustees with a view to purchasing their property in the Church, control over which they needed to carry out vital repairs. The trustees were evidently willing to sell only if at the same time they were able to dispossess themselves of the liability of the school and almshouses—they saw, no doubt, that they had a bargaining hold over the parish. Accordingly, an agreement was concluded that September, which entered into force in 1782, whereby the trustees conveyed all the church and charity property to the Vestry, in return for a reduction of the payment under the endowment to £21 per annum. This agreement was quite illegal—the Vestry had no right whatever to conclude it. They also had to compensate the almspriest-schoolmaster, Rev. Griffith Lloyd. He was granted an annuity for life of £20, and was to be allowed to retain his house in the foundation building. Lloyd took boarders, whom he lodged in the almshouse, and ran his school as a classical grammar school for them. The free school of eight boys was under a separate master, employed by Lloyd. This master took no Latin, but lessons in it were arranged if desired for the free scholars either by Lloyd, or a visiting master, at extra cost. This resembled the arrangements used in Chigwell School.

Lloyd, however, died before the transfer took effect; he was buried on 2nd March 1782. Thus the school came completely under the control of the parish, or technically, its nominated trustees. The senior churchwarden, Joel Johnson, was instructed to provide for lessons as best he could until a new master was appointed.

The parish then reviewed Monoux's ordinances. Most were re-enacted, but the requirements for prayers for Monoux's soul, and the provisions for obits, as well as certain requirements for the almspeople, were repealed.

As far as the school was concerned, many changes were put into effect almost at once by the parish. It augmented the endowment, and increased the numbers in the school to about fifty—30 boys and

20 girls. A mistress was employed directly by the parish for the girls. Clothing was provided by Joel Johnson, churchwarden, such that he might spot truants in the street. It was of a standard pattern, and from its design the foundation became known as the Blue School, as opposed to the Green School, a name applied to the Marsh Street British School, set up in 1789 by dissenters, when the Monoux master is reputed to have made derogatory remarks about non-conformists in his charge. In 1815, the number of girls on the foundation was increased to 30. The subjects taught were then not classical, although they must have been in 1792 when one William Parson matriculated at Cambridge, "from the Walthamstow Grammar School". Education was not entirely free, for 17s. 6d. to £1 a year was charged for pens, ink, copy books and fuel.

In 1815, to make new clothes for the children, four pieces of white kersey (a coarse narrow cloth woven from long wool) were purchased from Leach & Broadbent of 38 Throgmorton Street, London, at 98s. a piece. These were then dyed dark blue (for £7) and set (8s.) by Charles Green & Co. of London, twice pressed (6s.) locally by Elizabeth Mayhew, and made up into thirty boys' suits at a cost of £18, half by John Hicks and half by William York, both of Marsh Street. Each suit therefore cost just over 30s. For the girls there were purchased six pieces of "Superfine Long Ells" at 52s. per piece from Walfords & Green of London. The same firm carried out the dyeing in blue, the setting, pressing, burling, etc. for £2 11s. 6d. A month later Ann Maynard submitted a bill for £8 5s. "For making the Blue Girls Cloths thirty Gowns and thirty Peticoats including Linings and Trimmings at five shillings and six pence each suit". Each girl's uniform therefore cost about 17s. 6d. plus the cost of material for the petticoats, which was not recorded.

In July each year, the children of the School apparently enjoyed buns and wine. The quantities are not given, but the price was 5s. for buns and 10s. 6d. for wine.

In 1818, the return made by George Hughes, the curate, to the Commons Select Committee on the Education of the Poor stated that there were 60 in the school, the master's salary being £37 p.a., and that of the mistress was £20 p.a.

A meeting of the Vestry on 3rd September 1818 received a report of the school committee "that very general and serious complaints have been made of the great disorder and want of discipline which prevails in the Girls Blue School". The girls' teacher at this time was a Mrs. Abbott. It was found that "the present Mistress has not sufficient authority to restrain the ill-conduct of the Children". A resolution was passed that the mistress's resignation be accepted, and the school suspended.

On 10th September, Anne Maynard was appointed mistress "until the commencement of the school on the plan of the National Education Society". Part of the trouble seems to have been the overcrowding of the children, and after having thought about enlarging the schoolroom, it was decided to put up a new building (cost to be met by voluntary subscription) and to combine in it the Girls Blue School, the Sunday School, and some of the girls from the workhouse. Apparently, it was decided later to accommodate boys as well.

On 2nd April 1819, the Vestry met to consider an application for the grant of a piece of land belonging to the parish, tenanted by John Humphreys, in the yard adjoining the Poor House, to be used for the erection of a school for 100 boys and 100 girls "to be Raised and Maintained by Voluntary Contributions". This was agreed, and the new school was in use by the autumn of 1819. The site mentioned was at the eastern side of the workhouse acre, with the pathway across the Common (now Vestry Road) running between the workhouse and the school. The building (which still stands though no longer used as a school) contained accommodation for the master and mistress, and was enlarged in 1825. So the Blue School was separated from the Monoux foundation, and both continued independently, the former as the National School.

It is noteworthy, incidentally, that neither the Monoux nor Maynard endowments, nor any subsequent ruling, discriminated between boys and girls receiving the benefits of the school. The fact that education for girls was provided at all by the post-1782 re-organisation indicated the demand; but perhaps the lack of provision after 1819, when a higher course was re-instituted, demonstrates the lack of demand for anything but elementary education. Nevertheless, the intention of the Founder to provide for girls was recognised, even in 1884, when the Charity Commissioners' scheme made specific reference to the setting up of a Monoux Girls' School when funds became available. When the charity income was commuted to provide grants for further education, girls became eligible again for its benefits.

CHAPTER IV

DECLINE AND REFOUNDATION : 1820-1889

The trustees now decided to improve the status of the Monoux School. They advertised for a grammar-school master, able to teach the classical languages in accordance with the 1659 Commission and with what they conceived to have been Monoux's intentions. The person appointed was the Revd. F. Parsons, who lasted no more than a month or so, and he was replaced by the Revd. J. F. Roberts, who appears to have arrived in March 1820. He was previously Second Master at Felsted School, where the First Master, the Revd. E. Squire, had at that time (1813-29) completely run down the charity school provisions, and substituted a fee-paying boarding school of his own devising in the premises.

The name of Roberts has been much vilified, and some strange misconceptions have been accepted of the running of the school during his time, the most popular of which is that the numbers taught were reduced at one time to five boys. Roberts, it is certain, ran the school for his own profit. After his arrival, he changed the course of instruction, such that the boys then in the school were taught quite different subjects. He also increased the charges for extras to between 20s. and 44s. per year, with the result that most of the scholars left forthwith. From then on, he taught Latin and Greek free of charge, but made a charge of six guineas a year for instruction in English, History, Geography, Mathematics—the Felsted system, in fact.

Roberts therefore altered the whole outlook of the school. His real purpose was to take boarders, outside the foundation, and teach them, together with a few local boys, at a much more remunerative rate. He took a house in Church Lane, identified as the Walnuts, opposite the Ancient House. There he ran a boarding establishment, seemingly holding some thirty boys at any one time. Teaching took place in the building belonging to the foundation.

Of this period, we have a remarkable narrative by Edward Berthon, clergyman and marine inventor. He was the son of a London merchant with Walthamstow connections, who had become bankrupt. Edward was sent to the Monoux School in 1820, after a spell in a larger private school in Wanstead. He was nine at the time, and the youngest in the school. The boarders seem to have been ill-fed, and strictly taught, but Berthon himself later went on to Cambridge, as did some of his contemporaries. The schoolroom over the almshouses is described as "a wretched draughty loft, with a steep open-tiled roof". He describes a riot in the boarding house, and its consequences; Roberts threatening to flog the whole school, and after some hectoring, commuting the sentence to a thousand lines. One of

Berthon's memories concerns the long board, still in the present School's possession, reading "Georgius Monox, Eques, hanc Scholam fundavit, AD 1527", which he says "was nearly three hundred years old". If so, its inscription must have been renewed, for the "s" of "Eques" is painted as "f", in the style of the eighteenth century.

Roberts was doing no more than schoolmasters up and down the country were doing. Many a Tudor institution was converted into a reputable school by the same process; and he might have prospered more had he been less restrictive in the course of education offered to the free scholars. Something of the kind happened at Chigwell School, and at the Colchester Royal Grammar School, and these schools prospered greatly later in the century. As it was, his method of expanding the profitable boarding side at the expense of the foundation led eventually to his removal in 1836, shortly after the Charity Commissioners' Report.

Ironically, four years after Roberts had been dismissed, Parliament passed the Grammar Schools Act, which would effectively have deprived him of his basis for conducting the school. This was that the trustees, in appointing him, had stated that the school was a classical one, following the edict of the 1659 Commission, which he interpreted, whether in good faith or not, as an obligation upon himself to teach gratuitously only Greek and Latin, as was the case in many classical schools up and down the country. The Act of 1840 put an end to this, so that Roberts could have been required to teach English subjects free of charge also. In any case, the return the Parish made in 1833 to a Commons Committee states that Roberts was teaching fifteen in the Charity School, as well as his boarders, so obviously some effort was made to comply with the Charity Commissioners' ruling.

After Roberts came Thomas Waite, who in 1838 obtained permission to appoint a deputy. This was Robert Watkins, "late second master at Corrie's Grammar School, Madras". A prospectus of Watkins' time has survived, in which it is stated foundationers paid 2 gns. p.a. and non-foundationers, 4 gns. p.a. for day boys, and 22 or 25 gns. p.a. for twelve boarders, "including Washing, Mending Linen, and use of separate beds". There were about fifty boys in the school in the late 1830s. Waite left the school in 1842, and the Vicar of Walthamstow required of his successor, Dalton, the services in church prescribed in Monoux's will, which had fallen into desuetude. Dalton and his successor, Pennington, came to have less and less contact with the school. Indeed, in 1848, it appears that some teaching, probably divinity, was in the hands of a clergyman of independent means, Dr. Greig, of Walthamstow House. When Watkins departed, the trustees prohibited the taking of boarders, and numbers sank to twenty-five or fewer. For the last thirty years of the School's life in the almshouses, the master was Mr. Henry Griggs, a Norfolkman from Diss, born in

1809. During this time, the school usually had between fifteen and twenty-four pupils, in the age range nine to fourteen. Latin was latterly taught "when required"; and everyday work consisted of English, writing, arithmetic, book-keeping, geography and history. All were foundation scholars, unlike in most grammar schools, where the Roberts system prevailed. Lessons took place on Mondays, Tuesdays, Thursdays and Fridays, with half-days on Wednesdays and Saturdays.

The state of the schoolroom gave rise to continual problems despite alterations and repairs in 1814, 1834, and 1842. In June 1854, Mr. Griggs wrote a strongly worded letter to the trustees, complaining of decaying timber giving rise to noxious odours. He was still complaining about this in 1867!

In April 1866, the School was visited by an inspector from the Schools Enquiry Commission, which in 1868 presented to the House of Commons a comprehensive record of every anciently endowed school in England and Wales. The inspector, James Fearon, made some ambiguous remarks about the Monoux School's history in his report which have been perpetuated by subsequent writers. He tells only half the story about Roberts, says that only English was taught immediately prior to 1782 (meaning "no Latin was taught"), and mis-states the date of the Foundation. But his report of the school in action is very illuminating. For just as Roberts had advisedly contrived to defeat the ends of the Foundation, so had a combination of insufficiency of funds and maladministration in 1866 produced a school inefficient in three distinct ways.

First, Henry Griggs was not a graduate, nor was he required to be. The alms-priest **was** a graduate, as required by the 1659 Commission, but he did not teach in the school at all, for he had been allowed, or required, by the Vicar to appoint a deputy. The inspector did not openly criticise Griggs, but stated "(he) professes to teach Latin, Greek . . . and other subjects required for a liberal education", with the direct implication that he was not capable of teaching all those subjects.

Secondly, for no boy was the course gratuitous, as Monoux and Maynard had intended. Each scholar paid 4 guineas a year, some 8 guineas, and, additionally, books were 30s. per year. It will be remembered that Roberts had charged £6 6s. even in the inflationary times of 1820!

Thirdly, the results attained by the schools were of an extremely low standard; lower, Fearon said, than the second grade of many British or National (i.e. elementary) schools. The reasons for this were fourfold. Firstly, the master could not take boarders, for this the trustees had prohibited after Watkins' departure. So he could neither increase his own, nor the foundation's, income. Secondly, the

Forest School, opened in 1834, had become a first-rate and prestigious establishment, offering a course of education which for day-boys in 1859 cost only £5 p.a. more than that of the Monoux School, at a much higher and more professional level, which naturally attracted the sons of the middle class of the district. There was also a higher-elementary grade in the Walthamstow National School for poorer children. Thirdly, by insisting that the alms-priest be his curate, the Vicar had necessarily reduced the standing of the school, although he may with justice have thought the money better expended in that way. Fourthly, the income from the foundation was absurdly low, and the trustees did not, as some trustees of schools did, seek to augment the income by public subscription or any other method. Little responsibility could be attached to Griggs personally, who apparently to willing learners was a painstaking and thorough master in the most adverse of conditions.

The 1868 Report gave a number of interesting details. Griggs' daughter took the boys for drawing and possibly for French. She also ran a girls' school—presumably a small one—in the Monoux master's house. The average age of the seventeen Monoux boys was just over 11 years. More important, they had been in the school on average less than six months. Only three boys had been there more than a year. Griggs explained this by saying that most of his older boys had recently left, but even so, it goes some way to explaining the unusually low standards in the school at the time of the inspection. The inspector wrote acidly, "Into the attainments of the lowest class, I did not enquire".

The occupations of the fathers are interesting. One was a lawyer, the only profession represented (his son was in the infamous "lowest class"). Six were clerks, one was a contractor, and the goods agent at Snaresbrook Station sent both his sons to the school. The remaining seven boys were the sons of two coachmen, a tailor, a silversmith, two butchers, and a scientific instrument maker. The subjects taught were Latin (to three boys), Greek ("there is never any demand"), history, geography, arithmetic, book-keeping, French and drawing (to two boys and to one respectively). Griggs also claimed sometimes to teach German. Punishment was by caning "rarely used". The school was inspected twice a year by the alms-priest. Scripture was not taught as such, but the school day began and ended with prayers. In the immediate post-Roberts period, it is thought that the alms-priest continued to give religious instruction. Even this had ceased by 1868, though candidates were still prepared for confirmation.

We have few first-hand accounts of the school in Grigg's time, and only two by his pupils. A. A. Peacock, writing in **The Monovian** in the late 1920s, mentioned the slight ambition of most of the boys. He refers also to the high esteem in which Griggs was held, and to his extreme care and diligence with any boy who had the makings of a scholar. Peacock attended in the last years of the unreformed school. The other account comes, in 1936, from George Keable, who was at the school in the early 1860s, and apart from being a splendid, if brief, cameo of life in the old, rural, Walthamstow, is interesting in two ways. Firstly, he says that the school then was of "twenty or thirty boys"—which lends credence to Griggs' statement to Fearon that a large proportion of his boys had recently left. Secondly, he mentions that a favourite pastime of the boys was to pour water through the cracks in the floorboards so that it dripped on to the almsfolk below! One begins to doubt the wisdom of Monoux's dual provision for youth and age.

The question of whether girls were taught in the Monoux School after 1819 is a vexed one. Certainly they were not admitted to the foundation in the Roberts regime (1820-36), or the Griggs era (c.1850-1879). The origin of the speculation here was an undated local newspaper clipping in a school scrapbook of the late 1920s, which was an obituary for a lady who is stated to have "attended as a girl the old Monoux school by St.Mary's Church". Exact dates were not given, but her attendance must have been between 1858 and 1863. The probable explanation for this is that this girl was one of the private pupils of Mr. Griggs' daughter, noted by the inspector, Fearon, in 1866. Since Miss Griggs also taught some of the boys for French and drawing, it is possible that joint lessons were held. Since the boy foundationers were paying mandatory fees at that time, it is quite likely that the distinction between Miss Griggs' private pupils and her father's school became a fine one.

The first major attempt to reform the school appears to have taken place in 1870, when three factors combined to make the time opportune. Firstly, the office of almspriest-schoolmaster became vacant after George Hignett, a successful applicant for the curate's post, refused to accept the post. Secondly, Henry Griggs had obviously been heavily criticised through the report of Fearon. Thirdly, in 1869, the Endowed Schools Act had become law, which provided the means to the trustees of augmenting the endowment of the school. This was section 30 of the Act, which provided that, if certain conditions were met, the Endowed Schools Commissioners could make an order diverting to educational purposes the resources of under-used dole, apprenticeship, and miscellaneous charities.

Thus it was that on 26 April 1870, a group of the Walthamstow establishment gathered in the Vestry Room to resolve that the Monoux School be converted to "a middle-class school, for which there is great need in the Parish of Walthamstow". They then wrote to the Commissioners to that effect, mentioning several charities that could be appropriated under section 30 of the 1869 Act.

After the usual meetings, a draft scheme was agreed, and published in January, 1873. But this scheme, and an attempt to revive it in 1877, both failed because the governors of the charities to be diverted felt unable to agree to the terms, and their concurrence was essential for the purposes of the Act. There was also a certain amount of disquiet in the town. The Working Mens' Institute—one of whose officers was Henry Griggs—made objections, and very reasonable criticisms were offered by the normally-moderate **Walthamstow Chronicle** in its editorials in February, 1877.

Griggs' own position was precarious. If either of the plans of the seventies had been accepted, the trustees had it in mind to pension him. He would certainly have lost his job, because the draft schemes insisted the master of the reformed school be a graduate. He himself knew this, for a letter still exists in the school from him referring to the first meeting between the interested gentlemen and the commissioners in May, 1870, as "determining my whole future".

As things happened, it was a combination of Griggs' death, and the regrouping of all the Walthamstow charities under single direction, that led eventually to the refoundation of the school.

There is no record of the exact date of closure of the old school. Henry Griggs was paid by the trustees up to 25th November 1879. There is no exact record of his death, but Peacock says it was in 1879 or 1880. The Trustees were still advertising places in the school on 20 December 1879 and it is possible that a temporary master was engaged during 1880, but the school was certainly closed by 6th January 1881, when the Trustees leased out the rooms in the almshouse building.

Funds were then allowed to accumulate, the school being held in abeyance by virtue of a decision of the Charity Commissioners in 1880. On 9th September 1884, the Commissioners made a scheme which provided for the re-foundation of the Monoux School. This diverted the income of certain other charities to augment the Monoux and Maynard income, taking £130 per annum out of the Inhabitants' Donation Trust (a fund set up in 1650 which was endowed with a field to the south of Hagger Lane, and which had just been divided up, some parts let on building leases, and some sold to the Great Eastern Railway), and £50 per annum from Wise's Charity, a fund established in 1734. This fund was endowed with land in the Leytonstone Road, which had also in the 1870s been let on building leases.

The 1884 scheme was the first clear and unambiguous basis which the school had ever had. It laid down in considerable detail the aims and conduct of the charity. The Head Master was to be a graduate secured by public advertisement. The School was to be for day scholars only, not fewer than two hundred in number, between the ages of seven and fifteen. The upper limit was subject to raising in individual cases. Preference was to be given to Walthamstow boys. An entrance examination in reading, writing from dictation, and arithmetic, was to be held. Fees were set at between £3 and £6 per annum, but twenty free places were to be maintained unless more than 200 boys were being educated, when one additional free place for every ten additional scholars was to be made available. It will be remembered that Monoux had provided for free education for 20 or 30 children. Free places were to be awarded preferentially to Walthamstow elementary school scholars.

The Headmaster's salary was fixed at £100 and a house, and a capitation allowance of 30s. to £3 per annum for each pupil in the school. The Headmaster was superannuable at the Governors' discretion.

The school was to teach the following subjects: non-denominational religious instruction, reading, writing, arithmetic, geography, history, English grammar, composition and literature, mathematics, Latin, at least one modern language, natural science, drawing, drill, and vocal music. The arrangement of the timetable was left to the Headmaster's discretion. The school was to be inspected annually for its attainment and efficiency (in addition, the Board of Education held inspections from 1902 onwards).

The really significant factor of the 1884 scheme was that it allowed the school to expand. The old system had restricted its size and thus its efficiency. But by the 1884 arrangements, the demand for private education was to subsidise the education of the poor, in a much larger foundation. But because £180 per annum was diverted from the dole charities to the educational charity, the scheme laid the Governors open to later allegations that, in fact, the reverse was happening.

The school therefore re-opened on 14th January 1886 in the schoolroom in West Avenue belonging to the Trinity Congregational Church. The Head Master appointed in 1885 was Henry Allpass, a young man of 25, who had previously taught at the Bristol Cathedral School. He later entered the ministry, and combined his post with that of curate of St. James' parish. By the 1884 scheme, the Governors had been empowered to hire buildings pending completion of their own. At first, they had intended to use the house "Woodlands" near Wood Street, but the Endowed Schools Commissioners had objected. The site for the new building was in High Street and construction began in February 1889 to a design by W. Jacomb-Gibbon and J. W. S. Burmester, though the actual erection was less ornate than the plans owing to lack of funds. The foundation stone was laid on 13th July 1889, and the building was formally opened on 18th December 1889 by the Lord Mayor of London, Sir Henry Isaacs, though lessons did not begin there until 20th January 1890. It cost £4,095.

It is difficult to assess realistically the School's standing in its first years after re-foundation. Allpass most certainly was a popular and energetic master. Reports of the period which survive by disinterested visiting examiners are uniformly good—the mathematics and scientific side being especially strong. A chemistry laboratory was given by W. E. Whittingham, a governor, in 1892, which was a facility few schools possessed at that time. The social and corporate life of the institution seems to have been thorough-going; prize days, athletic meetings, and school outings being well patronised. The School Song, composed by J. F. H. Read, another governor, dates from 1890. Whether the school less than four years after its re-foundation really was a **monument of fame** from "England's shore to India's strand" is to be doubted, but the serious lesson of Read's words perhaps is that such a spirit of pride in the school did exist that the School Song's inaccuracies could be unflinchingly and enthusiastically accepted by its contemporaries. The Monoux tradition was then, as it is now, often glibly spoken about, but a school has a short memory, and a tradition is often more a product of ten years than of a hundred. We may accept, I think, that the first decade of re-foundation was one of solid achievement. It was the time when the school's precarious first 350 years, when its existence at all was often to be seen as an ineffectual fulfilment of the wishes of a long-dead founder, was consolidated into a really thriving institution. Between 1544 and 1886, the School could have closed at any time without many regrets. After 1890, its demise was unthinkable.

CHAPTER V

FINANCIAL CRISIS AND THE COUNTY TAKEOVER : 1889-1927

The re-founded school was further financed by a complex scheme of the Charity Commissioners, made in 1890. By it, the school was subsidised further by the diversion of funds from yet other Walthamstow charities, notably the dole charities of Rigg, Sims, Banks, Legendre, Collard, Harman and Bedford, and the Apprentice Boys' Charity of Mary Newell. These charities produced about £145 annually. There was a certain degree of opposition to the 1890 scheme from the town, led by J. J. McSheedy, a Radical, and perpetual opponent of the Walthamstow establishment. They accused the Governors of financial mismanagement, and certain of them, of open dishonesty. But behind this lay a total unwillingness to accept that money left to the poor of Walthamstow should be diverted to "educate the sons of gentlemen", as one of McSheedy's round robins dated September 1891 had it.

To this point of view there was certainly some justification. By the 1884 and 1890 schemes, there were to be about 25 free places at the school. On the basis, however, of the school fees at this time being £6 per annum, the income lost to the authorities was some £150. Over £300 per annum, however, was being appropriated from the charity account—£145 from those listed above, £130 from the Inhabitants' Fund of 1650, and £50 from Wise's charity. Thus there was indeed an effective subvention to the school from funds originally for the poor.

The social composition of the school in 1890, though not quite of a nature accurately to be described as "sons of gentlemen", was certainly not representative of the town as a whole. In 1887-8 no less than 67% of the fathers of boys admitted were in the professions, clerical workers, or retailers. In 1902, this figure was 79%. In the national census, these groups accounted for but 13% of Walthamstow's population.

It is worth mentioning here that, from the 1890's a number of Monoux boys were prepared for entrance to Christ's Hospital at the age of 13. Cambridge Local Examinations were taken, and a number of boys also sat for the Civil Service Third Division or L.C.C. Clerical Class examinations at the age of 14. There was no uniform, but during the 1890s certain boys wore a clerical type habit about which little is known. There was also a red and black cap, awarded for success in sport.

Sir Reader Bullard, a Walthamstow boy of the 1890s, who attended first Bancroft's School, and then the Monoux School, realised the root causes of the school's problems even whilst a pupil;

the lack of money, principally, and the comparative lack of scholarship of the staff. Bullard, it may be noted, though obviously a brilliant pupil in the elementary school he attended, failed the Monoux entrance examination, probably because of the number of subjects required, which then included shorthand or drawing.

H. A. Allpass was earning £500 per annum as headmaster when he resigned in 1903 because of ill-health. He recommended William Francis Spivey, the second master, to be his successor. The Governors acquiesced in the choice of Spivey, but took the line that they could no longer afford to pay him £500. They invited the Board of Education to concur in an open defiance of the 1884 scheme, by which the minimum salary permissible was £400. This the Board refused to do; but the Governors adopted an artful compromise, whereby they paid Spivey £500, but expected him to employ the woodwork master (at £100 per annum) out of his stipend. They also failed to advertise the post publicly as the scheme required. No doubt they saw this as a proper course in the circumstances, but it had the effect only of procuring a further existence for the school on the verge of penury. Spivey was always patently very highly regarded by all who knew him, whether boy or master, but in the light of subsequent reports it may be doubted whether he was as ideal a Head Master as the Governors obviously thought.

The state of the school twenty years after re-foundation is shown in several ways. The first of these are the Inspectors' Reports, the second is Michael Sadler's very thorough examination of secondary education in Essex, and the third by the various, and numerous, accounts of former masters and pupils. Of these, Sadler is probably the most valuable in placing the development of the school into the context of the times. By 1900, Walthamstow had grown almost to its optimum population. If we think, then, of the vast number of houses erected since 1900, we may envisage something of the social fabric of the town in the first decade of this century—a much larger family size, a much more densely packed population, predominantly young families. Most of these were skilled artisans—only 13% were professional, commercial and clerical persons, and less than 10% unskilled labourers. Because of the profusion of large growing families, the educational system had to be in a state of continual expansion; and a walk through Walthamstow even today will provide plenty of proof of the School Board's endeavours and success in providing elementary school places in the large, two-storeyed, neighbourhood schools.

Secondary education in the country as a whole was less well provided. The private entrepreneur was a common aspect of the system, with the large municipal, or county, higher school much less so.

The Monoux School had been re-housed in 1889, the plans having been drawn up some years previously. Between 1885 and 1910, Walthamstow's population had increased by 300%: the population under 15 years of age by an even greater percentage. Hence the accommodation had become inadequate. Moreover, the total income for school purposes was extremely low—£135 from the foundation, £365 in government grant, and £250 from the county, were received in 1903-4. Fees brought in just over £800. The physical and pecuniary resources were, then, very low. Some boys at the school at the time of Sadler's survey had come from the Council elementary schools (44%). Rather more had private primary education (53%). This again reflects that the 13% of Walthamstow's population engaged in professional and clerical work provided a disproportionately high number of the Monoux pupils.

This in part illustrates that secondary education was given a low priority in the accepted way of life for working-class children. It is largely forgotten these days that such families, often of six or seven children, could live adequately only if children were sent out to work at the earliest possible age. The chances of a boy in London and its suburbs gaining a scholarship to a secondary school were 170 to 1 in 1892. But the inhabitants of Walthamstow in the early part of this century were beginning to have rather higher aspirations for their children, and it is probable that real poverty in the town was low. Many of the artisan families could manage to keep their sons longer at school, through higher earning capacity. Sadler informs us that perhaps 75% of leavers entered the professions, the Civil Service, or city offices as clerks. The last named was the most popular, with only about 15% entering the Civil Service, and 7 or 8% the professions. Hence it is clear that the Monoux school offered, even in its condition in 1905, a means of social advancement to a middle strata of Walthamstow society.

The fees at the school were £6 per annum for the older boys, with an extra 24s. a year for books and the like. Only six or seven scholarships for the annual intake of 45 were available. These were preferentially awarded to boys from Walthamstow council schools.

Sadler's report on the school, if optimistic, was in general adverse. His main objections were to the inadequacy of the buildings and the consequent restrictions placed on the teaching. This was, of course, only part of the school's perennial problem—the lack of funds, which was probably at that time insoluble. Sadler's assessment of the teaching was also low, particularly of the arrangement of the curriculum. He argued that in view of the future careers of the bulk of the pupils, excessive time was spent on science and mathematics. The reason for this disproportion, was, again, the lack of funds. The Board of Education had a special grant available to secondary schools

The Monoux School and Almshouses next to St. Mary's Church, c.1900.

Sketch of the school and almshouses from George Monoux's Ledger c.1527.

Entrance to the schoolroom in the almshouse building. The stone reads "Grammar School founded by Sir George Monoux A.D. 1527".

Interior of the first schoolroom above the almshouses.

A staff group in the early days of the High Street building.

The architects' drawing of the High Street building.

The High Street building in its early days.

A lower form in the school c.1895.

Laboratory presented by W. E. Whittingham in 1892.

Aerial view of the Chingford Road buildings in 1927 or 1928.

The opening ceremony of the Chingford Road building, 20 July 1927.
[Daily Mirror]

Lower forms evacuated to Lucton, Herefordshire, in 1940.

A.T.C. Flight in 1943.

A Sports Day in the late 1930s.

A display at the opening of the new Sports Pavilion in 1961.
[Waltham Forest Guardian]

able to provide an experimental science course, and giving a certain standard of teaching in the subject. This was an essential part of the Monoux School's income, hence the timetable had at some time—probably in 1895 or 1896—been adjusted to provide the required amount of natural science teaching. In fact, the proportion of science teaching in 1906 differed little from that of the 1960s. By an accident of administration, the school's curriculum provided a modern (i.e. a post-World War II) subject balance in Edwardian times.

Sadler's solution was to amalgamate the school with the Technical Institute day school, which had been founded in 1897 by the then newly constituted Urban District Council. It was co-educational from the beginning. By 1905 it catered for just over 200 children, of which girls were in a considerable majority. In effect, it provided a four year secondary course at 11+, and at 13+ a two year higher elementary course. Again, there was a scientific bias to the teaching in order to earn the Board of Education special grant. Sadler was much more satisfied with the teaching which he saw as progressive and enthusiastic compared with the technique of the Monoux masters, which he regarded as outmoded and pedestrian.

Sadler was an advocate of single-sex education, and advised accordingly that the Walthamstow High School for Girls (of which he approved without reservation) should, in effect, take the Technical Institute girls, whereas the Technical Institute/Monoux amalgamation should be in essence a take-over by the former, with the Monoux name being retained for historical reasons, if it were thought desirable.

The first statutory inspection of the school also took place in 1906, and its findings closely matched those of Sadler. The conclusion of the Inspectors, though, was interesting. "There is so much that is good in the school, and it is so clearly capable of filling efficiently a most important place in the public provision of education, that it appears incumbent upon the local authority to secure to it . . . a sufficient income". The strongest subjects were science and mathematics; the weakest were history, art and French. Entrance Scholarships were at this time awarded on the basis of an examination held on the first Saturday in December in Reading, Writing, Dictation, Drawing, and Arithmetic; and three subjects from History, Geography, Grammar, Mechanics and Shorthand—which must have been something of a marathon! The Head Master stated that "scholarship boys pass through with distinction . . . some proceeding to the Universities".

In March 1907, the Board of Education threatened to withdraw its recognition of efficiency from the school, and its officers' minutes show clearly that this was an attempt to force the County Council into increasing their financial support[1]. A compromise was effected in June 1907 whereby the county paid for an additional master (at £125

---

[1]—First given after the 1902 Education Act.

per annum), but the Board continued to deny permanent recognition, in the hope of persuading the council to give a further subvention. After an increase of fees in 1910, the Board put the school back on a permanent recognition basis. But in 1913, another full inspection took place which was to have wide consequences.

Accounts of the school at this time as remembered by former pupils, like all such recollections, are tinged with sharp loyalty. There is no doubt the value of the teaching and school life were appreciated by the boys rather more than the accounts of Sadler and the Board's Inspectors would suggest. Despite the lack of money, school life was full. Games were played at various grounds in the town, the Forest was used for cross-country races and the like. Various concerts and socials took place, and a December prize-giving, at the Victoria Hall, predecessor of the Granada cinema. Most of the pupils found undoubtedly that the school gave them a good start in life; for many, it was obviously the starting point of much social advancement. An Old Boys' Club was formed and thrived, when such things were virtually unknown, such was the loyalty of the former pupils.

In 1913, a General Inspection of the school took place, and the report of the Inspectors was very poor indeed. Teaching was regarded as inefficient in every subject other than Chemistry. Spivey's direction of the school was characterized as deficient. Some quotations will supply the tenor of the report . . . "there is little to say in praise of the staff" . . . "the literature teaching was dull and slow" . . . "the teaching was most faulty, and made worse by a flood of irrelevant talk" . . ." The Inspectors sum up, "The atmosphere of the school is one of plodding industry. Its modest work is done without flagging, and without distinction".

The private notes attached to the Board of Education records of the 1913 Inspection are very interesting. One particular master was heavily criticised, and on the day after the inspection, Spivey dismissed him. The master concerned appealed to the Board of Education. The Inspectors thought Spivey had too high an opinion of the individual and collective worth of his staff, and framed some of their report with the intention of getting this across to him. They were particularly worried that "neither the headmaster nor any member of staff seems capable of stimulating interest . . . in clubs and societies . . . the whole institution lacks life and initiative". H. M. I. Barnett went further, and actually said in a memorandum that which can be read between the lines in the report, "I am inclined", he says, "to despair of any improvement whilst he [Spivey] is head, poor man".

Spivey himself reacted decisively to the Inspectors' report, and there exists a long and bitter comment by him, which the Governors accepted and supported without question, and which they sent to the Board of Education as a memorandum of dissent. The dissent was not ignored by the Board, but they took the view that both Spivey and the Governors were setting their standards far too low; and furthermore, that no amelioration could be expected with the administration as it was. Accordingly, on 29th June 1914, the Board formally indicated to the Governors their intention to cease to recognise the school as efficient. Since half of its income would be lost, the foundation had no alternative but to seek a take-over from the County. On 28th September 1914, the foundation approached the Essex County Council, and on 5th November the plans were approved by the Higher Education sub-committee. Just before this, Mr. Spivey suddenly died. The Board of Education then withdrew its notice.

So it was that Arthur Hall Prowse, the Second Master, was appointed Acting Head Master, to guide the school through a difficult time. Since he was not a graduate, he was warned that he had no chance of the permanent position which would occur when the county's plan of merging the Monoux School with the Walthamstow County High School for Boys came to fruition. The latter school was the Technical Institute, taken over by the Essex County Council by virtue of the 1902 Education Act, and renamed about 1912. Two reforms initiated by Prowse were the house and prefectorial systems (1915/6). Both of these had been orally recommended by the 1913 inspection. The houses were simply numbered at first from one to four. They were named shortly before the move to Chingford Road, and expanded to six. This was reduced to four again in 1974.

The staffs were amalgamated, and the two schools became one, in theory, on 1st September 1916. The County made additions to the High Street building at a cost of £1,400. These were a series of hutments made of corrugated iron, other materials not being available during the war. On 7th November 1916 the Essex County Council initiated an abortive Compulsory Purchase Order for the new site in Chingford Road, even before the High Street extensions were ready. In fact, the Hoe Street boys did not attend in the Monoux buildings until 7th January 1917. In December 1916, an unprecedented number (five) of new assistant masters had been engaged, and in the previous September a new Head Master, G. A. Millward, had taken up his post. The High Street buildings therefore became even more cramped. The school was not entirely taken over by the County in 1916. It occupied an odd status, according to the Board of Education, of "Independent School voluntarily controlled by the Authority". This lasted until 1920.

After amalgamation, boys were still admitted at the age of eight, though this was phased out just after the war. Christ's Hospital entrance took place until 1923. Gradually, however, 11+ became the usual entry age for the Monoux School.

Even before the amalgamation, in October 1915, a new school building had been decided upon. It was to be for 300, but capable of taking 400 if necessary. The site was finally bought on 23rd July 1919 and in October 1919 the Authority leased it to Mr. Hitchman for grazing cows since "no works were in prospect this growing season".

The period of amalgamation saw problems in the leadership of the school. G. A. Millward, the new Head Master, joined the Forces in May 1917, and until his demobilisation in January 1919, Prowse again led the School. Then Millward left in order to take up the headmastership of King George V Grammar School, Southport, and was succeeded by J. K. King.

September 1920 was a difficult period for a new headmaster to take up his appointment. The Geddes axe was in progress, and the promised new school seemed as far away as ever. The country was in the first post-war depression, with high unemployment and social and industrial unrest. King has all but been forgotten as a Monoux headmaster, but it was he on the one part, and the County Council's subvention on the other, that turned the school into a first-rate institution. The Cambridge Local Examination was rejected in favour of the London Certificate; the teaching of Spanish, and regular teaching of German (sporadic from 1912) were introduced. The Cadet Corps was disbanded, proper games and P.T.—the latter in hired halls—substituted. A wireless was installed in 1921 and used in a "senior course in civics and current affairs". Throughout the period, King constantly urged the Governors, and through them the Committee and the County, for better facilities, and prompt attention to the new school. He received few rewards for his pains. When in February 1922 he indented for a new carpet in his study, he was instructed to buy a rug to cover the holes! His salary (£500 per annum) remained static, whilst those of other masters were increased.

Nevertheless, for the first time the school started to attain results of a higher calibre. Between 1922 and 1925, eighteen scholars, mainly non-fee paying from Walthamstow elementary schools, went on to higher education, and six open scholarships were won. These are figures which may nowadays seem normal. Then, they were outstanding. Many of these leavers were aided by scholarships from the Monoux Foundation. This was the result of the Essex County Council's purchase, in 1920, of the school site, the purchase money, and other funds, being invested to provide leaving exhibitions for Walthamstow children at the Monoux and High Schools, together with two entrance scholarships.

In 1925, the Board of Education again inspected the School, and this time their report was as full of praise and commendation as that of 1913 had been of condemnation. Its conclusion was that "the school is well organised, and thoroughly efficient . . . there is work of a high order in several of the main subjects . . . and . . . no really weak spots . . ." The sixth form, however, remained small with only 16 boys.

The new building plans progressed slowly. There had been a dispute between 1916 and 1919 as to the site of the new school, during which the Board of Education and the Essex County Council had preferred the Chingford Road site, and the Governors had harried them in favour of a plot on the corner of Farnan Avenue and Forest Road, now the site of the County Court House. The economic situation prevented plans being drawn up before December 1922, when they were approved by the County. Working drawings were ready in October 1924, but at this point the Board caused certain readjustments, notably simpler elevations, to be made. Work started in March 1926, a tender of £42,626 having been accepted the previous September. Then the contractor withdrew, and direct labour was substituted. But work had been allowed to start before approval for a loan had been given, and this the Ministry of Health, who gave such authorisation, were loth to do, since Walthamstow (upon which fell all the interest charges in line with County policy) was already heavily in debt. It was not until 31st May 1926 that a letter was sent from the Board of Education to the Ministry of Health setting out the Monoux scheme as an urgent case, upon the personal decision, it is recorded, of the Minister, Lord Eustace Percy. On 10th June 1926, the loan was issued, and building began in earnest. The final cost of the land and buildings, including making up the sports field, was £52,138.

Some general observations on the school in its last years in High Street seem appropriate before considering the Chingford Road era. Firstly, the site itself had become more cramped. The temporary buildings erected in 1916, and the additional three classrooms of 1920/21 reduced the playground space virtually to nil. The comforts of the staff were negligible; at one time they had to share the Head's study. High Street between 1890 and 1927 had changed from a semi-rural thoroughfare with large houses, to a busy street market "of roaring costers" as one account had it. Gillard's pickle and pie factory stood across the road, without the barrier of shops erected later. The corner by the baths was the traditional place for revivalists, barrel-organs, and performing monkey shows. The Monovian of those days had a multitude of exotic sights, sounds and smells to distract him from his work. The staff-room had "a kind of warm fug . . . conducive to the telling of exceptional stories . . ." according to one former master. One wonders how long the 28lbs. of Rough Shag delivered in November 1923 lasted, for it, no doubt, provided the "warm fug". (Up to the war, Head Masters had a licence to sell tobacco to the Assistant Masters).

Other innovations of King's period were a revised prefectorial system, the regular **Monovian** magazine, the "Bust-up", or masters' and sixth form Social Club, and the naming of the Houses after school benefactors (to which Morris has always been an inexplicable addition). Between 1916 and 1926, it should also be stated, the Monoux school catered solely for Walthamstow boys. The differential fees charged were abolished in January 1921, but by that time the only non-Walthamstow pupils were those whose parents had moved out of the district since their admission, and the very occasional boy admitted by reciprocal arrangement with the London County Council.

King resigned in May 1925 to take up an appointment at the George Green School with the L.C.C. He was succeeded, after a term, by Harold Midgley, who came from St. Olave's School, where he was a housemaster. Midgley was a linguist, and had written text-books for German teaching. It was thus with a relatively new headmaster that the school took over its new premises, but it was undoubtedly through the solid achievement of the King era that its flourishing state was due.

From October 1926, the title of the school "Monoux Grammar School", then in general use, was officially changed to "Sir George Monoux' Grammar School, but locally the apostrophe was almost never used in the official form. The Board of Education continued to use "Sir George Monoux's Grammar School".

CHAPTER VI

'A BUILDING WORTHY OF THE FOUNDATION': 1927-1939

On 20th July 1927, the new school was formally opened by the Lord Mayor of London, Sir Rowland Blades, and was occupied from the following term. The teaching staff was augmented by two in the new school that September. The furniture and fittings cost £3,057, which the Authority took on loan.

Midgley caused a major upheaval in August 1927. When the Education Committee examined the lists of new entrants to the school who had been chosen by him and the staff, they found that 23 boys from the 81 who had been notified by the school of places were from outside Walthamstow—principally from Chingford, where there was no grammar school until 1938. There ensued a correspondence between the Walthamstow committee and the Essex authority, in which it was eventually decided to allow those who had been admitted to remain. After this, there was rather more supervision of the selection procedure, and non-Walthamstow boys were not admitted in any numbers for another five years.

The school buildings were incomplete at the time of their opening, and the gym/dining hall block were not completed until the 1931/2 school year. This is the very high building which closes the "E" of the main buildings, and became known as the "Bastille". It cost a further £7,000.

In June 1931 Harold Midgley suddenly died, and once more, Arthur Prowse became acting Head Master. To replace Midgley, the Education Committee appointed Percy Denis Goodall, previously Head Master of Falmouth Grammar School. One gets the impression that under Midgley the school's policy was one of results through solid, conventional, teaching—which undoubtedly paid dividends. Goodall, however, was something of an innovator. He had high ideals on the place of the school in civic and social life, and of education as a means to promoting good world citizenship.

Administrative changes also occurred. In 1932, primary control of the school passed from the Walthamstow to the Essex authority. The demand for places consequently increased. Indeed, the population of the whole south-west Essex area increased rapidly, and the Authority began building a new school at Buckhurst Hill to relieve the pressure on Monoux. But in 1934 and 1935 the school had to expand to 4-form entry (128 per year) to cater for the pressure. This put considerable stress on the available resources. In 1933 the system of 100% special places was adopted, and with it the 11+ Entrance Examination. The system meant that parents paid a proportion of the full fee (£21 per annum for Essex residents) according to their means. In 1935, 45% of the boys paid no fee at all, 23% paid reduced fees, and 2% the full charge. The last vestiges of fee paying disappeared after the passing of the 1944 Education Act.

From the 1930s, the "Monoux family" idea was encouraged. The Parents' Association was formed and fostered; the Old Monovians drawn closer into school life. More important, perhaps, clubs, societies and school visits were encouraged on a scale not before known, and the school's corporate identity established.

The Board of Education again inspected the school in March 1935, and reported in generally favourable terms, with one or two important reservations. Of these, the most important was the lack of an established sixth-form tradition. Only 25 boys from 525 were in the sixth, and even that number was on the decrease. An average of 8 boys per year took Higher School Certificate, and 4 went to a University. This no doubt was partly due to the recession in the country at large, and the wish of parents to find their sons secure posts at the first practicable opportunity, but it did little to foster high academic aims for the school. The Inspectors reported also on the scant usage of the new dining room, and suggested it be converted to a biology laboratory. This was eventually done. A certain degree of criticism was levelled at the unimaginative nature of the teaching, especially of the older members of the staff, but no serious lapses were detected. Praise was given to the history and German teaching, in particular; to the standard of oral expression in the school; to discipline; and to the prefectorial system.

Later in the 1930s, the teaching of Esperanto was started, reflecting the internationalist ideas of the Head. Another innovation was that of ju-jitsu, for which the school featured in a Movietone cinema newsreel. The late 1930s were also a time of the tremendous dramatic productions—"The Ghost Train" for some reason always occurring to those who remember them. And in the last summer of peace, a fete was held for the Education Assistance Fund, which realised the then huge sum of £600. That same summer, the cloisters around the quadrangle were bricked up at a cost of £904.

CHAPTER VII

EVACUATION : 1939-43

The onset of war in September 1939 had the immediate effect of totally disrupting the life of the school. Walthamstow was an evacuable area under the Government's regulations, though at first Chingford was not! The school was convened early, on Monday 28th August, when war was judged imminent. There followed a week spent waiting, which was occupied largely in games (the holidays officially continuing).

Evacuation took place on 2nd September, the school being accommodated in a special train from Black Horse Road Station to Ampthill in Bedfordshire. Ampthill is an ancient market town, but a very small one. The boys were billeted both in the town itself and in the surrounding villages of Marston Moretaine, Maulden, and Lidlington. Groups of boys, ranging from 45 to 100, were billeted in each place, and four or five masters accompanied each contingent. Attached to the party were the younger brothers (and sisters) of the Monoux boys. At Lidlington, the villagers were expecting a party of primary schoolgirls, and at Maulden (to quote from a contemporary account) "one master found himself doomed to share a solitary single bed with four others".

Lessons, from 16th September, took place in various church halls —in Ampthill, in the Wesleyan Chapel and the Union Chapel. Lessons were somewhat attenuated in scope at first, since there were no text-books, ink or blackboards. Evening, weekend, and in some cases, afternoon, activities had to be organised, and these took the form of walks, filling sandbags, helping local farmers, A.R.P., first-aid, and games, including one euphemistically known as "progressive table-tennis".

On 17th November, the school moved to Colchester. This time the evacuation was by bus. The idea was probably to re-establish the school as a single unit, in one place. No. 12 Lexden Road became the "Monoux House"—a place for storage of books, a staff and prefects' room, as well as a room variously used for classes and recreation. From Colchester, 48 miles from Walthamstow, many of the boys were able to cycle home for weekends and at holidays. It must not be forgotten also that many parents had recalled their sons, largely because of the lack of air raids in the early months of the war. In Colchester, the Monoux School worked in the Royal Grammar School and in various of the town's schools, and in the technical college. Success in examinations was maintained after a year of evacuation, though, of course in lower numbers. In Colchester, the boys found themselves in relatively familiar surroundings, and life seems to have presented a less rustic and makeshift appearance than it did in Bedfordshire.

However, the School moved yet again, this time by train from Colchester on 2nd June 1940, and arrived eventually in Bromyard, in Herefordshire. The move was occasioned, one suspects, by the fears of invasion, for a decision had been taken by the Government during the late Spring to make Colchester itself an evacuable area, and the date set for this was 1st July 1940. In Colchester, the School was billeted almost on the east coast. In Bromyard, it was in the rural Marches of Wales.

The Bromyard interlude lasted only a fortnight. Thereafter, the bulk of the school travelled by coach to Leominster, also in Herefordshire, but about 36 first formers were accommodated at Lucton School, about five miles from the town.

Leominster proved the longest stay, and when evacuation is remembered by former Monovians, it is to Leominster that their thoughts principally return. In early 1942, there were twelve masters in Leominster, including the one at Lucton. The number of evacuees was variable, but it reached a maximum of just under 200. Lessons were held largely in the town's small Grammar School, three full days a week, and half days on Saturdays and two other days. Holidays usually prompted a mass return to Walthamstow, despite official disapproval. A new Head Master, J. F. Elam, took office after Christmas 1941 to replace P. D. Goodall, who left suddenly. The reasons for his departure have never satisfactorily been made public. Mr. Emery, Second Master, took charge in the intervening period.

The School seems to have acclimatised quickly to Leominster life. There were two distinct views of evacuation; those of the evacuee and those of the host. Monoux memories of Leominster are varied. There were undoubtedly difficulties; in teaching, in being away from parents and homes, and in billeting. From the point of view of the townspeople, the infusion of 200 boys meant inconvenience and a disruption to the normal run of things. The organisation, for instance, of evening activities was of mutual benefit, releasing the hosts to something like their former privacy, and the boys to the companionship of their friends. In the end, the Monoux Social Club functioned six nights a week. The Leominster view of the school is not recorded.

CHAPTER VIII

THE POST-WAR GRAMMAR SCHOOL: 1943-1968

Just before Easter 1943, the School began to return to Walthamstow, and reopened in the Chingford Road building on 17th May. The library, staff-rooms, hall, and north corridors were at first still in use by the Army, and were not vacated until September. The large number of boys who had been attending schools for those not evacuated, whilst still officially allocated to Monoux, then joined the returned evacuees, and the school again reached 400 in size.

Before the move, the School had collected money to buy for the Leominster Grammar School a sports trophy. The sixth-form had held a farewell dance at a restaurant in the town, and it is a testimony to the friendships which had been formed that the **Monovian** was to record, a year after the return, that large numbers of boys and masters had gone back to Leominster during the summer holidays.

J. F. Elam was an historian, and something of an innovator. In 1943 he circulated to the staff a paper modestly entitled "Some thoughts on the Curriculum", which was in reality a thoroughgoing revision of the policies of the School, so that even today it presents a modern and progressive aspect. Elam wanted to expand the sixth form, for this he saw as the essence of a good school. He wanted to relate teaching much more to life outside School, to make it less rigidly confined to examination work, and to prepare boys for a responsible life "as citizens of a democratic country". He introduced a School Council as a way of inducing responsible participation; the election of prefects; and set out to encourage fifth form students to stay on into the sixth even if they did not intend to go to a university. In particular subjects, certain changes were also instituted. Esperanto was abolished, moves were mooted to unify science teaching, and remove the divisions among the three sections. Option choices were to be left open to a later stage. Local history and geography were to be introduced into the teaching of those subjects. Much of the scheme remained as the thinking behind the School's work until its dissolution as a grammar school in 1968.

After its return to Walthamstow, the School was still much disrupted. At Leyton County High School there was a sizeable Monoux contingent, still with its own identity, which had to be repatriated, and other Monovians had strayed into provincial schools. Some staff were in the forces, and others had been deployed by the authorities in various Essex schools. Senior boys were engaged in firewatching, an Air Cadet Squadron was established, and games were somewhat curtailed because of the state of the grounds. The school buildings had a narrow escape when two long range V2 rockets demolished houses on the opposite side of Chingford Road, and behind the school nearly adjacent to school field. After these incidents, lessons were held in the McGuffie school for a month or so.

The end of the war brought the construction of a kitchen/dining room block, and the replacement of the old dining room above the gymnasium by a biology laboratory. Many of the school's fittings had ben displaced, and some, like the lampshades in the corridors, took a very long time to reappear.

J. F. Elam moved on to Colchester Royal Grammar School in 1948 where he remained until the late 1960s. He was succeeded by Vincent J. Stirrup, who came to Monoux after a short spell in charge of the small de Aston Grammar School at Market Rasen, Lincolnshire. But despite changes at the top, the staff in 1955—about 28 in number, included some ten who had been at the school since the 1930s. The staff even now includes six appointments made in the 1950s or before, but the continuity of service of such men as F. G. West (1921-61), H. J. Hyde (1927-66), J. S. Durrant (1929-69), L. C. Belchambers (1909-53) has not since been equalled.

Under Mr. Stirrup, the school grew gradually in academic stature. It expanded in numbers from 1956 to 1960, mainly taking account of the post-war population bulge. The usual 3-form entry pattern had to be expanded to four in certain years. This placed a certain burden on the buildings, especially as far as games were concerned. The North Field—i.e. that between the School and St. John's Church—was taken over for football pitches, but the changing facilities were not expanded. Hence a self-help campaign was started, and sufficient money raised to provide new changing rooms and pavilion, to which was added a new gymnasium, provided by the Authority. Both were opened in the 1960-61 school year. Then sights were set on a swimming pool, which eventually materialised in 1966. A new small hall, fitted up for projection of films, and used as a music room, had been added in 1961. This was recommended by the Inspectorate in 1956.

Exchange visits with foreign countries had re-started in 1949/50, when the Lycée d'Angoulême participated, and, in later years, visits with Weilburg in Germany took place. From the early 1960s at least, in common with other Walthamstow selective schools, language assistants were appointed each year.

The 1960s particularly were years of high academic and sporting success for the school. The sixth form became very large, and the possibilitities of expansion of higher education facilities were quickly realised. The boys were made aware of them in every way. There were possibly several reasons for the marked excellence of this period : certainly sustained endeavour by the Head Master brought the school many advantages. So did a quite exceptionally able intake of young staff in the late 1950s, each of whom was able to fire enthusiasm in the boys, and communicate deep interest in his subject. Another factor was the change of intake area. After 1944, the school began to take boys from a very wide area, from as far away as Epping and Waltham Abbey, and particularly, many from Chingford; such was its reputation. Competition for entrance was to such a degree that the effect was to select a much higher proportion of very able children than to most grammar schools. Streaming was virtually abolished after 1961, though certain subjects were "setted", or banded, according to ability. A fast stream taking four instead of five years to "O" level was tried, and abandoned, in the late fifties.

It was a school which included boys from a diversity of backgrounds—probably a greater diversity than Walthamstow itself typically provided. Like many grammar schools, it tended not to include those from the very top or very bottom of the social spectrum. The Head Master once found himself reported in **Quote of the Week** in the **Sunday Telegraph** for having stated that if to aim at good standards was to produce snobs, then it was his intention and design to produce snobs. But in reality, neither the policy or atmosphere of the school, nor the social realities of the town, were conducive to snobbery, whereas both tended to encourage the pursuit of high standards—sporting, academic, and social.

It was thus to a flourishing institution that the 1968 re-organisation, on comprehensive lines, of Waltham Forest secondary education came. Walthamstow, which was semi-autonomous from Essex in educational matters, was merged from 1st April 1965 into the Borough of Waltham Forest, together with Leyton and Chingford, which was vested with full County Borough powers in education.

CHAPTER IX

COMPREHENSIVE EDUCATION: 1968-1977

The idea of the comprehensive, or multilateral school, was not a new one. It was considered by, and strongly recommended to the Spens Committee of 1933/8, but rejected in favour of the tri-partite system by the Education Act of 1944. During the 1960s, it became Labour Party policy to promote comprehensive education, and in 1965 local authorities were instructed by the Ministry of Education to provide plans for comprehensive reorganisation soon after the accession to power of the Labour Government.

The Waltham Forest plans were submitted by a Labour Council, and approved in 1966. They provided for the abolition of selection after the 1967 intake. The 11+ examination had been abolished in 1965, and thereafter selection was carried out by reports from primary schools. Under the reorganisation plan, the Monoux School was to remain single-sex, but to become a senior high school—that is, a school providing places for boys from 14 upwards, irrespective of ability. At first, some boys of low ability could elect to remain in the junior high schools, i.e. the existing Secondary Modern schools. After the raising of the school-leaving age to 16, this meant a two year course for all boys, followed by a sixth form course for those who could profit from it. Numbers would eventually increase from 600 to 1,000.

The proposals were, it is fair to say, regarded with much hostiliity by many of those connected with the School, but the objections were over-ruled. Shortly before the change-over, a Conservative Council gained power, but the plans went ahead. The name of the School was unchanged except for the deletion of "Grammar"; alone among Waltham Forest secondary schools, the suffix "Senior High" was not added.

The five years after reorganisation saw many changes. A science block was erected on the former tennis courts. In the main building, the library was removed from its panelled room in the centre of the upper floor to the old junior Chemistry laboratory. More important, Vincent Stirrup retired in the 24th year of his headmastership. This is not the place to enter into judgement on Mr. Stirrup's career at the Monoux School. It must suffice for me here to forecast that the writer of the 500th anniversary resume will find the years 1948-71 ones of exceptional vigour and achievement.

The present Head Master is Mr. A. Brockman, himself an Old Monovian—the first time this has happened, and a rare event in any school. A fairly large number of Monovians have returned as masters over the years, and this supply shows no signs of drying up. The present time sees building contractors in the premises again. There have been few occasions in the last twenty years when no contractors have been present. Despite the ever-increasing numbers of appendages, the building from the front appears much as it did in 1927. The poplars round the grounds, subscribed for by Old Boys at 2s. 6d. each in 1932-3 give a distinctive appearance; as do the fine gardens tended by the caretaking staff.

Changes in the syllabus and scope of teaching naturally followed the reorganisation. More facilities were provided for the teaching of practical subjects, and for those boys who were academically less able. Many more ancillary staff have been provided in recent years to cope with routine jobs which once had to be done by the teaching staff, and to help with innovations such as audio-visual equipment. The house system has been developed into a pastoral structure. There are now two deputy head masters.

The growth of the comprehensive school has, however been to some extent, a natural evolution from the grammar school of the 1960s. It is difficult to observe recent developments in an historical context, but I think it is becoming clear that the 1968 change was not as final or as destructive as many people at the time thought—and certainly not as drastic as the changes that occurred sometime during the parish's control; or in 1820; or after Griggs' death. One can be sure also that the present will not remain long unchanged itself. As this book goes to press, the Government has issued a green paper on the educational system; the idea of the abandonment of sixth forms in schools, and the setting up of a 16+ college system has been mooted, and discipline, educational attainment, and teacher training are all being vigorously questioned. Since the mid-eighteenth century in the history of Monoux's school, there has hardly been a period of twenty-five years when some fundamental change has not taken place. It has typically and promptly reflected educational and social thinking in the country at large for 450 years, and will no doubt continue to do so—in the history of the school, **status quo** are words with but transitory meaning.

Perhaps, by coincidence, the buildings and their surroundings symbolise more of the history of the school and of Walthamstow than does the complex history of education in Monoux's foundation. Firstly, the almshouses, though changed by bombing, and surrounded by more modern buildings, suggest still the unchanging rural Walthamstow of the School's first 350 years. Second, the High Street building, except in the days of its infancy, surrounded by commerce, industry and urban toil; the product of a vastly changing town, whose population doubled with each census. Then, the large Chingford Road site, made in the time of Walthamstow's northward suburban expansion, on an altogether more spacious scale. Every salient point in the Monoux

School's long history reflects to some degree the development of society, whether in Walthamstow, or in the country at large. It has survived, despite many vicissitudes, because on the whole it has adapted to them. The history of Monoux's School shows varying fortunes, between mediocrity and excellence. If an institution can learn from its past, the school has many a homily, both of examples to follow and to avoid.

ACKNOWLEDGEMENTS

Many people have helped me with the preparation of this monograph. I have been particularly indebted to His Honour Judge A. E. Holdsworth, Q.C., H. W. Hebbard, Esq., A. T. Brockman, Esq., Robert Holden, A.I.L.A., and to W. G. S. Tonkin, Esq., an indefatigable typist. The loan of photographs is individually acknowledged. I am indebted to Bosworth's various accounts (W.A.S. 1st ser. nos. 3, 17, and 19) for the brief sketch of Monoux's life. Bosworth is also the only source for certain of the records of the school, which have now unfortunately been lost.

APPENDIX I

Monoux School Almspriests and Head Masters

Note : Most anciently endowed schools have few records of their masters. The list which follows is by no means complete, but it is more complete than could be derived for many schools. Where identification of a master with his degree is not absolutely certain, bold letters are used.

Almspriest-Schoolmasters

Name	Dates	Degree and University
John Hogeson	**fl.**1548	— **(Cantab.)**
Thomas Coleby	**fl.**1599-1609	
Robert Yarner	**fl.**1617	
Leonard Taylor	**fl.**1621-3	D.D.(Oxon.)
John Dawson	**fl.**1629	
William Groome	**fl.**1635	B.A.(Cantab.)
Thomas Aaron	**d.**1673	
Alexander Walker	**fl.**1699	
Charles Tough	**fl.**1714	B.A.(Cantab.)
Matthew Tate	**d.**1720	B.A.(Cantab.)
Thomas Colby	**fl.**1728	**M.A.(Cantab.)**
Alexander Cunningham	1740-62	M.A.(T.C.D.)
Griffith Lloyd	1762-82	B.A.(Cantab.)
John Harris	**fl.**1818	**B.A.(Cantab.)**
Frederick Parsons	1819	B.A.(Cantab.)
James Ffoulkes Roberts	1820-36	M.A.(Cantab.)
Thomas Waite	1837-42	**B.A.(Lond.)**
James Dalton	1842-5	M.A., L.Th.(Dunelm)
Arthur Pennington	1845-51	M.A.(Cantab.)

The following are listed by Bosworth in W.A.S. (1st ser.) 17, p.20. Neither dates nor forenames are given, and the source is not known.

Cain, Davies, Cook, Mattocks, Lewis-Forbes, Johnson, Ford, Birdsey, Vanderleer, Moody, Carter, Briercliffe, Archer, Mills, Gawthorne.

Headmasters

Name	Dates	Degree and University
Robert Watkins	c.1838-49	None
Henry Griggs	1850-79	None
Henry Alfred Allpass	1886-1903	B.A.(Lond.)
William Francis Spivey	1903-14	M.A.(T.C.D.)
George Alfred Millward	1915-20	M.A.(Cantab.)
James Kirkman King	1920-5	M.A.(Cantab.)
Harold Midgley	1925-31	B.A., B.Sc.(Lond.)
Percy Denis Goodall	1932-41	B.A., B.Sc.(Reading)
John Frederick Elam	1942-7	M.A.(Leeds)
Vincent Jackson Stirrup	1948-71	M.Sc.(Liverpool)
Allan Thomas Brockman	1971-	B.Sc.(Lond.)

Acting Headmasters

Arthur Hall Prowse	1915, 17-19; 31	None
Arthur George Emery	1941	B.Sc.(Lond.)
Arthur Jenkins	1971	B.A.(Wales)

Almspriest-schoolmasters during the headmastership of Henry Griggs, who did not teach :

Revds. McCape (1852); Boddy (1853-5); Knight (1855-8); Woolley (1858-62); Jones (1860-2); Elliot (1863-6); and Hill (1867-9).

APPENDIX II

Sources Used

PUBLISHED MATERIAL

Bullard, R. W.: **Camels Must Go** (1961).
Berthon, E. L.: **Retrospect of Eight Decades** (1899).
Leach, A. F.: **English Schools at the Reformation** (1896).
Goslett, P. H.: **Education in the Second World War** (1976).
Alumni Cantabrigienses, Alumni Oxonienses, and **Alumni Dublinenses.**
Sadler, M. E.: **Report on Secondary Education in Essex** (1906).
Spens Report on Secondary Education (1938).
Reports of the Charity Commissioners, Essex—Walthamstow (1832). (County set in the House of Commons Library).
Select Committee on the Education of the Poor (HC) 1819, IX pt. I.
Endowed Schools Return (HC) 1865, XLIII, p.45ff.
Schools Enquiry Commission Report (HC) 1867-68, XXVIII esp. pt. IX.
Secondary Education Royal Commission (HC) 1895, XLIII/XLIX.
Census of Population 1851 (HC) 1852-3, XC.
Select Committee on the Education of the People, (HC) 1834 IX; 1835 VII.
Victoria County History of Essex esp. Vol. II.
Royal Comm. Hist. Monuments (Essex) (1921).
Vestiges esp. Nos. 29 and 68. (Vestry House Museum).
Walthamstow Antiquarian Society **Monographs** (1st series). Nos. 3, 17, 19.
The Monovian (1926 to date).

UNPUBLISHED & MSS MATERIAL

Charity Commissioners : Schemes relating to the Foundation of 1884, 1891, 1896, 1901, 1907, 1911 and 1920.
Letters, documents, cuttings, etc. by permission of Mr. A. Brockman, headmaster, and Mr. V. Stirrup, former headmaster.
Walthamstow Charity Deeds (V.H.M.) uncatalogued.
Monoux Box (V.H.M.) uncatalogued (includes evacuation papers).
Walthamstow Higher Education Sub-Committee Minutes.
Essex Education Committee Minutes.
Commissions for Charitable Uses (17th Century) in the P.R.O.
Records of the Board of Education and H.M. Inspectors of Schools (P.R.O.).
Reports of H.M. Inspectors of Schools (V.H.M.).
Census Enumerations, 1851 and 1861 (Central Library, Walthamstow).
Robinson, W.: Collections . . . for an . . . account of Essex, Pt. II. (Central Library, Walthamstow. It contains a prospectus of c.1842).

NOTES ON THE ILLUSTRATIONS

Front Cover—The western wing of the Almshouses/Grammar School building in St. Mary's Churchyard from an etching by W. S. Longmore, 1878. The school was in the upper storey, and the master's house was in both storeys of the centre gable. (Courtesy Ian Shaw, Esq.).

Back Cover— The signature of George Monoux from the ledger in the British Library, and the form of his arms used by the school up to 1950, and since 1973, as a crest.

1—The school wing of the Churchyard building in about 1905. The Royal Commission on Historical Monuments stated that much of the elevation was rebuilt about 1700, though the west end wall was original. The whole of this wing was destroyed by a bomb on 8th October 1940. (V.H.M. collection).

2—The original plan from Monoux's Ledger for the school/almshouse building. The plan, which is not to scale, is a fairly typical Tudor drawing, with roofs shown in plan, not simply a crude sketch. It will be seen that the west (school) wing had a single-storey ground floor extension, and the school entrance was to be fitted up with a porch (the projection at the bottom of the drawing). The master's apartments were in the central transverse wing on both floors. (British Library photograph; Add. MS. 18783).

3—The grammar school wing from a photograph of c.1910, showing the entrance to the school, and an old inscription above it. At one time the staircase was external. (V.H.M.).

4—Interior of the west end of the old schoolroom photographed in 1915. Note the plastered space on the wall, on which quite possibly the wooden board, still in the school, recording the date of foundation ,was fixed. (H. V. Hopwood, V.H.M. collection).

5—Revd. H. A. Allpass (Head Master 1886-1903) seated to the left of his six assistant masters, probably in 1895 or 1896. W. F. Spivey (Head Master 1903-14) is on the right in the Trinity College, Dublin, gown. (V.H.M.).

6—Architects' drawing of the new school in High Street. Note the high windows and elaborate entrance, abandoned for a much less ornate design. (From the "Building News" 1889).

7—This photograph is supposed to be of the High Street building, on its opening day. This, however, cannot be so, as the school was opened in the depth of winter, and in the photograph there are leaves on the trees! In reality, it possibly dates from the mid-nineties. Note the difference between this photograph and the architects' drawing above. (A. J. B. Ward, V.H.M. collection).

8—Revd. Allpass with one of the lower forms and its form master c.1895. The boys in the frock coats are probably free scholars, but little is known about their costume. (Courtesy Head Master).

9—The laboratory given by W. E. Whittingham in 1892, pictured c.1895. Few schools had such facilities at that time. (Courtesy Head Master).

10—An aerial view of the Chingford Road buildings soon after completion in 1927. Note the old cottage to the left of the Porter's House, demolished in 1931 or 1932 for road widening. (V.H.M.).

11—The opening ceremony of the Chingford Road building on 20th July 1927. The Lord Mayor is to the centre of the table. The person speaking is Mr. Hewett, for the Education Committee. Among others on the platform are Mr. Midgley (Head Master) and the Bishop of Barking. (Daily Mirror photograph).

12—Some 36 Monovians of the lower forms, with one or two masters, spent much of their evacuation at Lucton School, Herefordshire. They are photographed here in the summer of 1940. (Courtesy Head Master).

13—During the war, and for a few years afterwards, the school ran a flight of the Air Training Corps. The Commanding Officer was Mr. Alfred Ninnim, the P.T. master. The flight won several awards for its proficiency. (Courtesy A. F. Ninnim).

14—A sports day in the late 1930s, showing boys and parents. Note school uniforms. (Courtesy A. F. Ninnim).

15—The opening of the new Pavilion, subscribed for by boys and parents, in the summer of 1961. (Waltham Forest Guardian photograph).